THE GREAT LAKES COTTAGE BOOK

The Great Lakes

COTTAGE BOOK

[THE PHOTOGRAPHY *of* ED WARGIN & ESSAYS *of* KATHY-JO WARGIN]

Sleeping Bear Press

Sleeping Bear Press
310 North Main
P.O. Box 20
Chelsea, Michigan 48118
www.sleepingbearpress.com

Printed and bound in Canada by Friesens
10 9 8 7 6 5 4 3 2 1

Library of Congress Cataloging-in-Publication Data
Wargin, Ed.
The Great Lakes cottage book / by Ed Wargin and Kathy-jo Wargin
p. cm.
ISBN 1-886947-66-X
1. Great Lakes Region--Pictorial works.
2. Cottages--Great Lakes Region--Pictorial works.
3. Great Lakes Region--Social life and customs--Pictorial works.
I. Wargin, Kathy-jo. II. Title.
F551. W27 2000
977--dc21
00-025954

TO MY FATHER, THE LATE RICHARD D. NELSON, WHO LOVED OUR little cabin on Hill Lake in Hill City, Minnesota. It was a small red A-frame set near a shore that was more swampy than firm, where the bugs were always bad and the zapper never worked, where one year a freak of nature brought hundreds of frogs to our deck and lawn overnight, where our fat beagle would always swim through green smelly crud during the dog days of summer and then jump onto our laps, and during the summer I was 14, it was where you always had to spend your afternoons rowing to the middle of the lake to pull me in, stroke after stroke, because I kept tipping over our Sunfish sailboat and could never tip it back. We all know that when you got cancer and we had to sell the A-frame when I was 16, that no one would probably miss it as much as you and I.

— Kathy-jo Wargin

To my lovely wife. I hope that someday I can buy back that cabin—or one like it—just for you.

— Ed Wargin

INTRODUCTION

WHEN ED AND I BEGAN THIS PROJECT, OUR FIRST QUESTION was, "what is a cottage?" What parameters will we use in deciding what is a cottage and what isn't? It was the toughest part of our assignment....where to begin, and how to end.

Our answers kept changing. Our ideas kept spinning. The conversation on the topic never slowed for what seemed like months.

Was a cottage a simple structure set in the woods, visited by few and seen by fewer? Or was it an elaborate home setting on the lakeshore, with banks of windows and pathways that twist and turn from the doors to the lake.

So when we set out, we asked ourselves what was the one thing that ties all of these places together, unifies them and sets them apart as what people have come to know as a Great Lake cottage?

And then we found our answer.

It was pride. It was the people. It was genuine affection for the Great Lakes. It was their care and willingness to open themselves to friends, family, and even friendly strangers. It was the fact that all of the cottages, camps or cabins on the Great Lakes were built with a longing to preserve cottage life, to enjoy it, and to share it with others.

It was the fact that the beds were made with quilts that covered generations of cottage-goers, that the faucets didn't always need to work because the lake water always felt fine for a bath, and that the kitchen was the place for conversations about nothing at all as well as for peeling potatoes and slicing lemons for tea. What it came down to was this: The cottages of the Great Lakes Region are about love of family and friends.

We hope you enjoy this book, *The Great Lakes Cottage Book*, as much as we did creating it. We have not disclosed exact locations of cottages, so that we may guard the privacy of the wonderful cottage owners who so graciously opened their homes to us, and shared their wonderful thoughts about cottage life with us. They are the best of the best, and they represent many of the wonderful kind-natured people who enjoy life on or in the Great Lakes region.

A classic cottage sits above the Lake Michigan shoreline near Harbor Springs.

Vines and a flag decorate one of the exterior walls.

Many sunsets have been watched from this outdoor deck.

A lantern and rope hang in an outdoor shoreline deck.

An inviting cottage rests peaceably in northern Michigan.

Flowers greet the morning visitor for breakfast.

The carving in the mantel tells of a wonderful legend from this historical resort area.

The perfect room for morning coffees, newspapers and delightful conversations about nothing at all.

A beautiful lakeside cottage waits for its guests.

Dinner this evening will be overlooking Lake Michigan.

A good book and a cold glass of ice tea suit this chair perfectly.

An arrangement of flowers greets the evening guests.

This bedroom lulls you to sleep—sweet, soft, summer sleep.

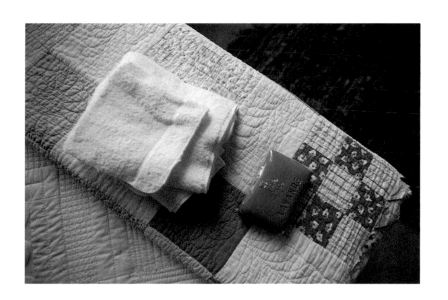

Soap and towels are ready.

Fourth of July—The height of summer!

A simple straw hat tops this cottage mirror.

The sun drenches the screen door with brilliant color.

HELLOOOOO! I HAVE SEVEN JARS OF BLACKBERRY JAM AND TWO brown paper bags of tomatoes for you...hello, are you there?

A familiar voice radiates through the worn metal screen of the back door. And then, the cottage door opens with a noise heard thousands of times before. It's the creaking of a rusty spring being pulled in the summer heat, its coils and chain expressing every bit of tension, ready to snap if pulled too far. And just at that moment when it sounds like it might, it rumbles into a quick swish of air and the hollow hitting of wood upon wood.

The door bounces back a time or two, each time sounding lighter and lighter as it settles back into the frame. As it does, it signals to all inside that someone has just arrived...at the cottage.

For many, the sound of their cottage door being opened and closed is as unmistakable as their own child's voice, ringing through the years with the good, the bad, the joyful, and the unforgettable.

Through its way the oldest of friends and the newest of neighbors have passed. It has been opened slowly on warm spring mornings when the grass is first starting to green. It has been slammed shut quickly on hot summer nights when moths are thick on its face. It has been tossed open wide by eager children as they rush in and out with freezer pops in one hand and a beach towel in the other.

For many families, as the children grow, the door will open less and less. And then one day those children will reappear at the cottage door as adults with children of their own.

Hellooo, they may call through the old metal screen, I have fresh rhubarb, the car ride was long, can you hold the baby?

And the sound of the cottage door with its rusty spring and tense coils will still be the same, signaling to all inside that someone has just arrived...once again, at the cottage.

Summer breezes stroll through the screen.

One of the many historical summer homes in the Bay View Association neighborhood.

White and green, classic cottage colors.

THE ASSOCIATION

THERE ARE MANY PRIVATE ASSOCIATIONS OF COTTAGES around the Great Lakes region. Some, like Bay View on Little Traverse Bay in Petoskey, which was founded as a Methodist Summer Camp in 1875, are open only during the summer months. When Bay View began, it was little more than a couple of tents, but ultimately it grew into a community of more than 400 Victorian style homes by the end of that century. Today, some of the goals of the association are to promote art, education, and recreation to its summer visitors. A walk through the streets on a summer night finds sweet notes sailing through the air as live music pours from its theater. And nearby, adults walk arm in arm as they did generations ago, while games of croquet and badminton are played out on the lawns.

Ready for any occasion.

A vintage Canadian trapper cottage relocated to north of Harbor Springs.

Timeless craftsmanship.

A stone walk leads you to the cottage door.

The woodpecker doorknocker announces your arrival.

A stone fireplace to warm the cottage on cold breezy days.

Memories stay forever on the fireplace mantel.

A cottage from yesteryear overlooks Lake Michigan.

A bar of soap waits outside.

Favorite collectibles decorate the fireplace.

The cottage door trimmed in blue.

Rustic furnishings create a warm nostalgic mood.

A sleeping loft is the perfect place for bedtime stories about bears, fish, birds and lakes.

Sun sets over the dock of a northern lake.

IT'S A LONG WALK TO THE DOCK. FROM THE COTTAGE IT DOESN'T look as long as it feels, edging its way down the hill and through the pines to a small bit of blue at its end.

But it's a satisfying long walk. It winds and turns, taking you downward in a rather steep manner, like an old switchback in the Alps. Walking such a path to the lake can be a time for closeness, each step providing the rhythm to accompany the perfect after-dinner conversation. Typically, it happens when two people start down the path, towels over their arms and long shirts over their swimsuits.

Pretty out today.

Sure is. Some storm last night.

Sure was. Watch your step.

I will. Sure is steep.

Yes it is. Stay on the path—poison ivy.

I see. Jack-in-the-Pulpits growing.

I know. Berries are ready, too.

That's great. Careful now—there are roots.

The conversation continues with the descent, thigh muscles tingling and hearts pounding. It goes on with each step, a little breathier-sounding and a little bit louder. And just then, when the lake is reached, the conversation comes to a drastic halt. The orange ball of sun sinks into the sky; the silver-smooth sheen of the lake reflects its warmth onto their faces. They take a few deep breaths to catch up with themselves. A fish jumps. Once. Twice.

Did you see that?

Fish?

Yes, twice.

Big.

Sure was.

Nice night isn't it?

Sure is.

Should we go back up?

Not yet. In a moment...

And with those few words, words that take place haltingly upon a winding path down to the lake, more is said about life, love, and being together, than any face-to-face conversation could ever produce.

A long winding path through the woods leads you to the dock.

Tranquil evening breezes from Lake Michigan cool off the warm summer days.

Rustic details lie everywhere in this cottage.

Shadows play on screen windows.

An antique lamp gently lights up the room.

THE LONG WALK ON THE BEACH

THERE ARE MANY REASONS TO TAKE A LONG WALK ON THE beach. A first date. A sorrowful goodbye. A father and son talk. An urge to quiet down and listen to our own voice, the one that speaks from somewhere deep inside.

And with every step, our foot sinks just a little bit into the hard-packed and wet sand, and the water licks our heels just a bit. All the while the smell of stale lake grasses and musty shells surround us, and we walk on, step after step.

And we listen. Because a long walk on the beach tell us one of the most important things in life. The more quiet we become, the more we will hear.

Sand gently glides through your toes at this beach on the end of the Old Mission Peninsula near Grand Traverse Bay on Lake Michigan.

The sun rises on a new day.

A cottage reflection.

This cottage rests just above the water's edge.

Sometimes there are no words to describe a moment, such as one spent on a screened porch.

SETTLING IN

IN THE LATE 1870S, RAILROADS BEGAN TO STRETCH NORTH FROM urban cities such as Detroit, and Chicago, as well as East Coast states. They made regular visits to the reaches of northern Michigan, bringing visitors, new residents and cottage goers. Summer colonies were built as people escaped the urban life for a week or two, or maybe even the entire summer. In many families, steamships carried the wife and children up north, where they would arrive, leather steamer trunks in tow, and long thick cotton dresses swishing as they walked. And there they would stay, to pioneer through the summer and create a life that would endure for generations.

This cottage echoes its Scandinavian heritage styling.

A wonderful combination of fresh air and natural light.

Have hat...will travel.

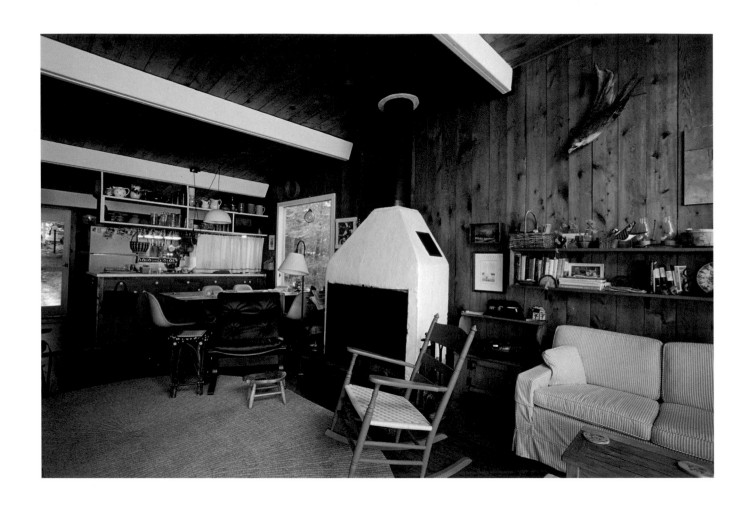

Easy summer living.

A summer cook is a busy cook.

The cottage is just around the corner.

THE DRIVE UP NORTH

IT'S FOUR-THIRTY FRIDAY AFTERNOON. THE CAR IS PACKED with two coolers, four bags of groceries, three duffel bags stuffed with swimsuits, towels, sunblock, and rolled-up beach balls. Three kids, two grown-ups, and one dog.

You do a double check for your license and the bait bucket you need to return to your neighbor at the lake—and you go.

As you roll out of town, you turn on some music—something relaxing, your co-pilot tells you—so the drive through the metro area doesn't get to you.

For a few miles, the car is filled with the notes of Mozart, the laughter of children, and the opening of snack bags. And then it happens. Someone takes on a serious tone and asks the one question that everyone is thinking but no one dares ask.

How long until we get there?

From that moment on, you are not just driving to the cottage, you are taking the long drive "up North."

Birch trees stand guard.

An open door to an old ice house where the shadows of birches play.

How many miles of water have these paddles traversed?

An array of life preservers wait.

.

LAUNDRY DAY AT THE LAKE

IT'S LAUNDRY DAY AT THE LAKE. CLOTHES ARE SOAKED IN A TUB of lake water, soaped and rinsed, then wrung by hand and hung on the line. Each pin is set strategically to ensure a full day of hanging. If the day is warm and the sun is high, the clothes will dry by the end of the day, stiff but clean, with the smell of the lake.

Like patient soldiers, these laundry pins wait for their next assignment.

Towels dry in the warm breezes from Glen Lake, in northern Michigan.

A bounty of ferns cover the ground surrounding this cottage.

A peaceful nook in the cottage gives solitude to the weary traveler.

This dock walks into paradise.

Daisies highlight the summer garden.

The perfect combination, gentle summer winds and a gentle summer novel.

THE BOOK

THERE ARE CERTAIN FRAGMENTS OF TIME AT THE COTTAGE remembered by the books that were read. The summer of *Undaunted Courage*. The week after the fourth of July which was spent reading *Blue Highways. For Whom the Bell Tolls* read from cover to cover three days before it was time to leave.

There are books about romance read in a quiet nook when the kids are out fishing. Books about mystery and intrigue that are taken in when the rest of the family is out for a bike ride. Pages with words that ease your eyes into a lazy nap. Stories that keep you up on hot summer nights when chirping crickets are the only sounds you hear.

These special times are about more than the plot and the characters. They are about the smell of the pages, the way the book felt in your hands as you held it close, and the way it looked on your table in the soft light of day. It is more than just a story, somehow, the memory of the book becomes the story of your summer.

Little footsteps press down the grass as they trail off towards the dock of a Glen Lake cottage.

A gardener's wooden pail, hose and watering can—this is the cottage of a green thumb.

THE GARDEN

A GARDEN AT THE LAKE BEHOLDS SWEEPING BEAUTY, FOR THE shapes and colors of the flora are lit against a backdrop of blue and green. And for many cottage gardeners, the joy is in the arranging of the bulbs, seeds, and starters, the nurturing of the first visual signs of success. And, the joy is also in the waiting.

The waiting, the watching, and the wishing.

And as the wishes are made, the morning glories, lupines, roses, pansies, and tiger lilies fill the mind's eye with their patterns. Simple desires that appear in the form of beautiful color.

Wishing for a garden at the lake is wanting a place that shows a summer of diligence and care, a fragrant spot to toss cares aside and simply sit for a moment or two. And when that garden comes to be, it is a place so beautiful that no one can help but to stop there and make some new wishes. And hopefully, they will be wishes worth waiting for.

Northern Minnesota gardeners make the best of their short growing season.

A picket fence gives way to the color of late summer flowers on Lake Ontario.

Flowers spotted through the screen door of a cottage near Cross Village on Lake Michigan.

RAINY DAYS

THERE IS A CERTAIN CLOSET IN EVERY COTTAGE. MOST OFTEN IT is dark and narrow, and a little musty inside. It can be found at the end of a long hallway or tucked behind a bathroom door. It's the type of closet no one ever really wants to go into, because it's dusty and disorganized, the door is warped and hard to open, and beyond that, the mouse traps are kept in there.

But there are days when that closet must be entered. It happens when the cottage is full of kids and the sky looms dark with an oncoming storm. It happens with the twink, twink, twink of the first raindrops as they pelt the windows. Then, and only then, someone dares to open that door.

Within moments the sound of cardboard boxes being pulled out from beneath other boxes fills the room. Plastic checkers rattle, marbles roll, puzzle pieces fall upon the floor until finally, the all-time cabin favorite is found and the box is pulled out. Metal pieces chink back and forth and pastel pieces of money stick out between the bottom and top cover.

I get to be the car! someone hollers.

And then, as the thunder rolls overhead, the wind blows and the rain beats hard, chaos erupts.

I get to be the thimble! You are the shoe, Mom can be the...

The initial commotion ceases when the board is set and the money is dealt. Everybody finds their favorite place to sit and Mom delivers cheese puffs and chips in plastic bowls, and sets out five bottles of grape soda. For the rest of the afternoon, the storm stalls overhead, lightning flashes over the lake, and waves crash along the beach. Everyone is satisfied to let the rain and the thunder carry on, because inside, it's time to let the games begin.

Rain dances along the surface of the window as the picket fence outside of this Crystal Lake cottage waits for tomorrow's children to play beside her.

We'll leave the lights on for you.

The definative sun porch.

Typical of many older cottages, several beds in the upper level are meant for summer visitors.

A small cottage holds big memories.

From times past stands an outhouse.

PICKING SHELLS

COLD GRAY MORNINGS ARE EXPECTED ALONG THE SHORES OF the Great Lakes. Roaring waters pound the beach, sending white-caps toward shore while clouds darken the sky.

These days are perfect for picking rocks and shells.

There is an art to the search, however. First, you bring along a small bucket and a large picnic blanket. The bucket is for the treasure, the blanket is for your lunch. Then as you find your way to a remote arc of a bay, you take off your shoes and roll up your pants.

And dig in.

Plink, plink, plink. Shells are discovered, agates are unveiled, and souvenirs made by Father Time and Mother Nature millions of years ago are brought home in the pocket of a toddler's dungarees.

The moon pokes its white nose through the fence during a stroll on Lake Huron's Sturgeon Bay at the tip of Michigan's thumb area.

Picking shells along the Great Lakes can be just as fun as picking them along the ocean.

A long winding path to solitude in a Great Lakes heartland.

The fields and woods hold many of natures best decorations.

The cabin!

This rustic interior holds charm.

As expected, a warm pot of coffee waits in the cabin.

A THOUSAND ISLANDS NIGHT'S REST

SLEEPING SOUNDLY IN A BUNKHOUSE, THE VISITOR WAS having an ideal night's rest. Days had been spent on the road, traveling the Great Lakes area, and with a weary and tired mind, he barely knew where he was.

He had fallen asleep around ten o'clock, only moments after he crawled into the oak-framed trundle bed.

The last thing he remembered as he drifted off were the stars through the window and the sound of the water rocking back and forth upon the shore.

And then...

Chug chug chug chug. Chug chug chug chug.

He sprang up in bed, disoriented and confused, the entire window filled with the side of a passing ship. No sky. No stars. Just the gray-white hull blocking his view.

And then he remembered—the 1,000 Islands are known for that.

The 1,000 Islands area, which is a 60-mile stretch along the St. Lawrence River at the mouth of Lake Ontario, is an area of large and small rocky islands, most of which are close to other islands and have cottages or homes on them. Freighters pass through frequently on their way to and from the ocean, dwarfing the islands and the homes, but adding nightly thrills for an unsuspecting guest or two.

A ship slips through the narrow channels of the St. Lawrence Seaway as it pushes toward Lake Ontario—only a few short miles down the way.

Sweet light intensifies this 1,000 Island cottage.

The sunset slowly walks down the staircase.

The 1,000 Islands area is home to hundreds of quaint boathouses like this one.

Many boathouses hold some of the most exceptional wooden cruiser boats in the entire Great Lakes region.

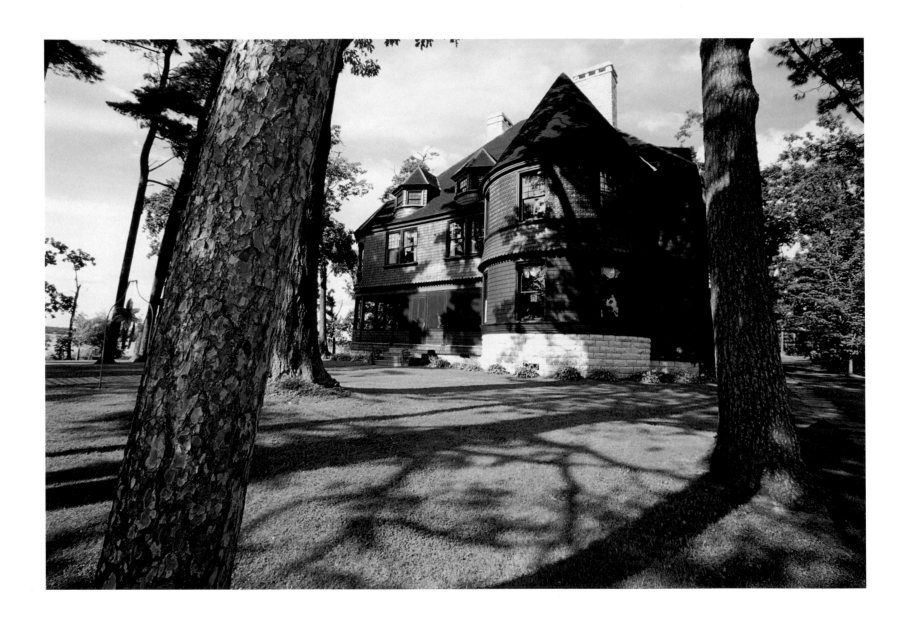

Many cottages date back to the late 1800s, and like this one, are so very, very grand.

A water spigot is an essential tool for the island gardener.

The round sun porch beckons for late afternoon ice tea.

An elegant staircase winds itself into the interior of this island cottage.

A grand dining room with fireplace.

A classic fishing cottage in the 1,000 Islands region.

An old paddle painted with the date it was made.

THE LURES

THERE ARE FISHING LURES ON THE WALL. OLD WOODEN lures with rusted hooks. Painted lures with shiny tines. Colorful chub lures, daredevils and crawlers. Spinners and rapalas. They hang from small nails, tinkling about in the breeze when the window is open, catching the sunlight as they move.

A collection like this tells a story about life on the water. Specifically, life on a river. In the 1,000 Islands area, there is a clear distinction between those who have made and spent a life on the water and those who merely visit. It is easy to recognize those who have steered their skiffs across the water with knowledge and experience. It is easy to distinguish those who have learned how to pack their boat and load it single-handedly in the worst weather conditions. It takes no effort to identify those who can guide their boat gently and safely around the stones that lie in wait just inches beneath the water. It is easy to recognize these people who have opted for inner strength over outside beauty. You just have to peek inside their cottages. They are the ones with fishing lures on their walls.

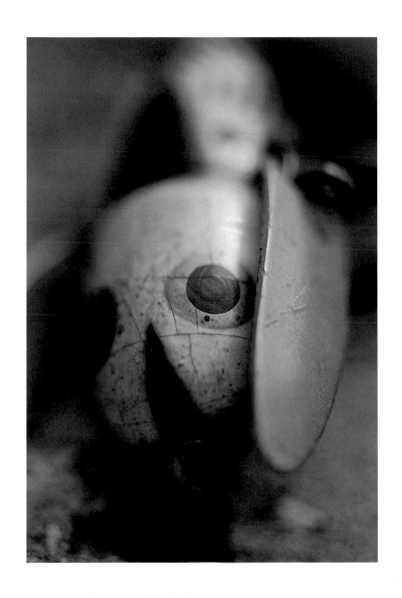

Fishing lures decorate the inside of the cottage, and fishing stories decorate the dinner conversation.

A single cottage fills most of this small island.

This tub is so deep that you can wash your children's hair while they're standing.

Perched on the rocks is a vintage cottage from the 1800s.

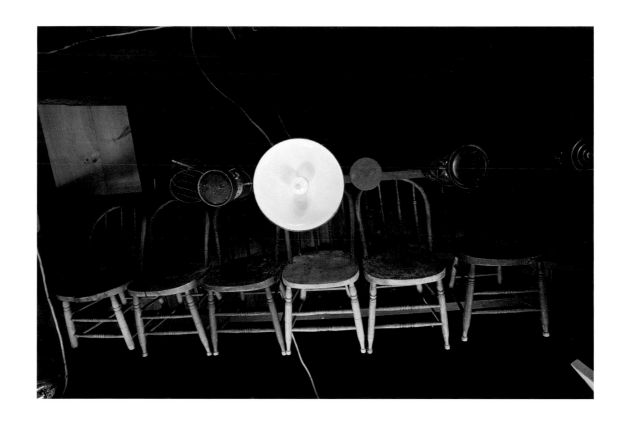

From the ceiling of the kitchen hang several wooden chairs.

In the cottage, even a bowl of fruit is art.

The distorted reflection of a side chair in an antique mirror.

A reflection of the breakfast area in a cottage mirror.

On the windows ledge rests old spice jars.

Blueberries are in order for this mornings breakfast—island style.

COTTAGE SCENT

FOR MANY FOLKS, THE SCENT OF A MOMENT CAN LINGER IN THE memory for years—if not a lifetime. Such beautiful smells will often spur us to relive a single cherished moment. The smell of a newborn baby's sweet head, the leather gloves dad wore every time he chopped wood at the lake, the perfume Mom only wore on Sundays.

It is no different for each cottage or cabin. Each has its own particular style, and its own particular smell. Some are sweetened with woodsmoke. Some are pungent with overtones of pine and cedar. Some are left a little stale by old rugs and dusty furniture, while others smell a little musty from years and years of wet beach towels on the couch, beach sand in the carpet, and soggy shoes left on the floor.

But regardless of the aroma itself, the idea is the same. That a simple smell can transport us back in time, and each time the door is opened and we take one long deep breath, we realize it's more than a wonderful or funky smell, it's a lifetime of memories in the air.

A perfect cottage setting in the 1,000 Islands of New York positioned gracefully on the St.Lawrence River.

THE GUEST BOOK

NAMES WRITTEN IN A GUEST BOOK DECADES AGO ARE NOW a blur of ink and dust. Names of who visited when and with whom, who brought what and what the temperature was. Names and initials of who danced with whom at the firemen's ball, who likes leeches more than minnows, who went to college and who went to work—and who never returned from the war.

Simple entries fill page after page, year after year.

In most guest books, the names do start to fade after awhile. Generation after generation of summers, some moments are lost amidst the blurring dust of the fading pages.

But this is where guest books are magical.

When a name fades from a page but the face remains clear and unchanged in our memory, we learn who meant the most to us— we learn who has left their imprints in our lives. The favorite niece who drove up from Cincinnati to announce her engagement in 1944, the neighbor three cabins down who died planting his prize tomatoes in 1956, the young boy with reddish freckles who lived at the lake year-round and never wore shoes and eventually married your daughter in 1960, and the fat old man with bib overalls who smelled like fish and cigars and sang vaudeville tunes in the talent show of 1972.

Such memories defy an old tattered leather-bound book; such memories defy the aging process altogether because adoration and love keeps them as crisp and clear on the day we die as the day they were made. For many of us, our heart has a guest book all its own.

A guest book from the 1,000 Islands region dates back to the mid 1800s.

This boathouse rests upon one of the many lakes that comprise Canada's Muskoka lakes area.

A red framed bed peeks through the window of this Muskoka cottage.

Utensils proudly hang in a Canadian cottage kitchen.

A typical wooden lake cruiser found in the Muskokas.

Morning light wraps this Muskoka cruiser.

A BOATHOUSE RESTS COMFORTABLY OVER THE WATER. INSIDE, A wet, wooden walkway wraps itself around the family boat, where the water slaps up at its sides and sometimes, over your shoes.

Boathouses became an integral part of Muskoka history in the early to mid 1900s. Because of the lakes and islands and waterways that create the area, passengers needed their own family boat available to transport them to their cottage. Many families built a boathouse over the water for that purpose, and most added guest quarters or servant chambers above the boathouse.

Today, boathouses are still an important part of Muskoka color. When you are in one, you can almost hear the voices of the people who used them generations ago, echoing from the walls and beams.

"Will you meet me back here at the boathouse later tonight?" asked the slim young gentleman in the tweed cap.

"I don't think I can; my parents might not like it" said the young school teacher of age 21, back to her beau.

"But the moon will be full and the water will be like a mirror—I promise they won't mind. Anyway, I have already asked them, and they said it is fine."

"You did?"

"Yes, so please don't be late; tonight I have something very important to ask you...."

And so we learn that it wasn't always about the boat, or the wooden walkway, or the water dampening our shoes. Sometimes it was about the romance of the lake and the moonlight as it appeared back then through the windows of the boathouse on a warm summer night.

Inside the boathouse, one of the three boats that were safely docked for the night.

FIRST LOVE

A GHOST OF A PATH LEADS FROM ONE COTTAGE TO THE NEXT. It is green and narrow and overgrown, but when the sunlight shines softly through the canopy, you can see what it once was— part of a summertime rite of passage—a familiar pathway made from the footsteps of first love.

Summer romances are like flames that flicker away through time. The path between their cottages is where they meet to steal a midnight kiss beneath the pines while fiddlehead ferns tickle their legs. It is where they wait to see each other, to exchange notes and souvenirs from the fair. The path becomes wider as the young love blossoms. A late night swim, hands held tightly in the moonlight, names written in the sand, early morning canoe rides to the far side of the bay.

Such pathways grow deeper and more defined through summer— wider and neater—connecting two old cottages and two young hearts.

And it will be on that path in the warmth of the summer evenings where they will laugh, they will love, and at summer's end, they will part. But they will never, ever forget.

A path between two cottages exists in many places, upon many lakes, and in many hearts. It is there to remind us all of sweeter and more innocent days, it is there to remind us how first love comes to be. Because first love in the summertime is like a path etched out of the forest; it is a trail made between hearts. As we grow older, it may become overgrown and narrow, but it is still there underneath it all, a path that is neat and wide. And upon it, in the lush summertime of our memory, love itself will linger on.

A pair of white Adirondack chairs linger in the memory of summertime romance.

Large stone steps greet visitors from the lake side of this Canadian summer home.

The perfect setting for relaxing on a summer afternoon.

Below the cottage rests a beautiful boathouse.

A yellow canoe waits to be paddled around a pristine Canadian lake.

35 degrees below zero in remote Canada.

No matter how cold it is outside, oranges will still ripen inside the cottage.

THE CUTTING OF ICE

SOME TRADITIONS ARE KEPT ALIVE FOR THE ROMANTIC notions they impart. Others are held close out of necessity.

There are some, however, that are a little bit of both. Like the cutting of ice.

In an area so remote it defies any map, ice is needed for refrigeration purposes, and must be cut and stored properly to ensure that it lasts all year. The task begins by shoveling a square patch of snow off a frozen lake. Imaginary corners of a square are marked, and an ice auger drills down through the ice in one of the corners. Then, a line is cut with a gasoline or hand-powered saw. The ice is cut from one corner to the next, and then another line is drawn. Eventually, the blocks are cut in segments of approximately one foot by one foot. As they float like white boats in an ocean of water so cold it's black, they are grabbed with massive tongs.

And then the fun begins.

The heavy chunks must be loaded, one by one, onto some type of sled and hauled to the icehouse where they are stacked and packed with layers of sawdust and snow.

There is something refreshing about hard work in subzero temperatures, especially when you are working with ice and cold water and wind on your face. Your body works a little bit harder, your nose and eyes and cheeks begin to feel cleansed by frost. And when the work is done, the food tastes better, the cabin feels warmer, and your muscles feel every movement you made. And somehow, next summer, the ice will taste better in a glass filled with the memory of that work.

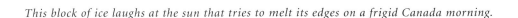

This block of ice laughs at the sun that tries to melt its edges on a frigid Canada morning.

Ice tongs save the day for the ice handler...as long as he or she doesn't drop them into the open water!

To this day, refrigeration for a remote camp like this relies on cut lake ice.

Warming steam rises above a small river in Canada.

THE BONFIRE

MANY ANCIENT CULTURES GATHERED STONES AND PLACED THEM in circles as a way to represent a place of spirituality as well as place of magic and wonder. Some cultures even placed fire in the middle. And these places of enchantment were used for storytelling, healing, and dreaming.

No doubt a bonfire can do the same.

It typically starts with a casual invitation—"hey, how about a fire tonight?"

Later, a small pit is created, shovel after shovel full of dirt, and lake-washed rocks are gathered and dropped around the circle's edge. When the dinner is finished and the dishes are washed, the kids have changed from their half-wet shorts to long pants and sweatshirts, friends and neighbors gather around the flames which move from yellow to orange and back again against the night sky. Smoke stings their eyes and weaves its way into their clothes. Stories are exchanged about how many minnows were caught with bare hands and who has the oldest aunt in the metro area. As the stars shine and the marshmallow bag is emptied, the smell of the night clings to each sweatshirt and windbreaker, casting a spell of enchantment all its own. Maybe this is what happened in those ancient stone circles, maybe it was not so much about mystery and intrigue as it was about simply enjoying a really nice bonfire.

A winter bonfire warms the face and the spirit.

Fallen leaves grace the ground in front of a Canadian cottage.

Before the sauna or in the mornings, a wash in the lake will wake any soul.

Stoking the fire is the primary charge for the seasoned sauna person.

THE SAUNA

LOYLYA VELJET LOYLYA. STEAM, MORE STEAM!

Fiery air seizes your lungs and captures your attention as you enter the sauna. Almost immediately, it soothes your muscles and clears your head. The scent of cedar permeates the room and your stress begins to assuage. There are two benches, one high, one low, and a bucket of water with a wooden ladle setting nearby. Outside, the air is crisp and the water in the lake is very, very cold.

Steam, more steam!

Saunas have been a part of cottage and cabin life in the northern areas of the Great Lakes for a very long time, especially in the far reaches of Canada and northern Minnesota. The date of origin for the sauna has often been questioned and can hardly be answered although the concept of sweating as a way to achieve cleanliness was used by many cultures. Most anthropologists will agree, however, that the Finns always had some type of sweating box or ritual. For them, in an area that had brutal outdoor conditions, it was the simplest way to keep clean. The Finnish sauna became popular when the Reformation made other types of bathhouses — which suffered from ill reputations as places for undesirable behavior — become nearly obsolete.

But why did the Finnish sauna endure when most from other cultures went by the wayside? One theory is that the people of Finland had a saying, and that was "in the sauna, conduct yourself as you would in church."

At the cottage, camp, or cabin, inviting your neighbors for a sauna is one way to get to know them better. If they are of adequate Scandinavian descent and feel they know you pretty well, they just might sit on the top bench, buck naked. If not, they may wear swimsuits or have some type of towel strategically placed upon their body.

Whatever you do, let them go in ahead of you, so you have the chance to peek in and see what the rules are. Otherwise, an embarrassing situation just might occur. Because rules for the sauna are the same as the rules for life—no one wants to be the first one naked.

An Ontario cottage window opens to a new day of fishing.

THE SUN ISN'T QUITE UP YET, AND NEITHER ARE THE CHILDREN. The kitchen fills with the smell of fresh coffee perking on the stove and cinnamon rolls baking in the oven. Grandpa steps lightly around Grandma, careful not to get in her way.

Then, as if the moment had been rehearsed a dozen times or so, Grandpa walks into the sun porch and reaches for the dusty orange life jackets.

One, two, three, four, five....

Soon, the cottage kitchen is alive with the sounds of five young children gathering silver breakfast spoons, bright blue plates heaped with scrambled eggs, bowls of ripe berries and whole white milk.

It's time to go fishing.

The children down their breakfast quickly. They bring their plates to the sink and step outside to find their shoes.

As they wait, Grandma opens an old bureau and takes five sweaters out of the bottom drawer. She passes them out, each sweater much too large and smelling of mothballs and cedar. Grandma insists they be put on right away, saying a big old smelly sweater is perfect when the morning is cool and you're in a boat fishing for walleye and northerns.

And then, with life jackets tied snug around their waists, they march in one straight line to the dock. Grandpa carries the red metal gas can. The oldest child right behind him with two extra oars in case something happens with the motor, although Grandpa says it has been fine since 1968. The others follow, one with poles, one with minnows, the next with a bag of candy bars and

eight cans of soda. The last and smallest child never carries anything, because they have all they can do just to walk without tripping over the roots that stick out in the dirt path to the dock.

Then, when everyone is arranged in their seats, Grandpa gives a pull.

One, two,three!

The smell of gasoline lingers for a moment or two as the boat putters away from the dock and past the next few cabins.

Grandpa smiles and raises the throttle. Five children with fishing poles, wind in their hair, beat of the waves pounding through the floor of the aluminum boat.

It won't matter if anybody catches anything. It won't matter if it's a little too cool or a little too warm. And it won't matter if the minnows don't live very long in the bucket.

When it's fishing day, no one really remembers how many fish were caught or how many fish got away. What everyone remembers is the smell of the lake water and how good a candy bar tastes in a boat. What everyone remembers is that Grandpa never gets mad when all of the lines are snagged on the same log at the same time, and the funny stories he tells about the old man who lives six cottages away and likes to steal inner tubes.

When the day is over and everyone piles into bed all tired and windworn and satisfied, what everyone remembers about a day spent fishing with Grandpa has very little to do with fishing, and everything to do with Grandpa.

No time to waste, the fish are jumping on the other side of the lake.

A Northern Pike makes for a satisfying campfire meal.

Grandma's rain slicker waits inside.

THE NORTH SHORE

THE COMPLETION OF THE SAULT LOCKS IN SAULT STE. MARIE, Michigan in 1855 made transportation from the eastern Great Lakes to Lake Superior much easier. Steamers such as the Illinois made pleasure excursions through the Great Lakes from places such as Buffalo, Cleveland, Detroit, and Chicago. It stopped at all the major ports around the Great Lakes on both America's and Canada's shores. Steamers like the Illinois brought many passengers to Duluth, Minnesota, and from that point, some would take local boats all the way up the north shore of Lake Superior.

In 1871, as Lake Superior saw an increase in passenger travel, a line of steamers called India, China, and Japan, otherwise called "The Triplets" were built especially for the route to Duluth. Many a traveler took the journey on one of the 235-foot iron liners at a ticket price of around $26.

The small passenger service that ran up the North Shore was the catalyst for the resort industry that exists there now. By the year 1900, the small towns of Lutsen, Hovland, and Grand Marais all had cabins and returning visitors.

Rugged shoreline south of Grand Marais, Minnesota.

A quiet harbor of sailboats in Grand Marais.

This view from this window has seen every weather pattern possible...and that was just today.

A Thompsonite covered fireplace is the centerpiece of the bedroom in this wonderful cottage.

A cottage in northern Minnesota near Lake Superior.

MOSQUITOES

IT IS PREDICTABLE. IT HAPPENS JUST AS THE SUN BEGINS TO SET. It happens when the day was warm and overly still. And it always seems to happen after the picnic table is set with its vinyl cloth and wicker plate holders. The swimmers come in from the lake and sit down with wet towels around their bodies. The others take off their sandals to let the grass tickle their feet. And just as the plates are filled with burgers and corn on the cob and potato salad, you know it's going to happen.

Ouch! Slap.

OOO! Slap.

AAAH! Slap. Slap.

Let's eat inside!

And then like clockwork, the summer suppertime brigade begins.

Plates and silverware are whisked inside along with opened cans of pop and one ketchup bottle, as everyone heads indoors and as far away from the little biters as possible.

Mosquitoes and lakes just naturally go together. It's the price paid for living in such beautiful and bountiful surroundings.

But all is not lost on those nights when the mosquitoes come out. Inside each cottage, decks of cards will fly as games of five card stud and gin rummy begin. Old magazines will be found under the bed and read from cover to cover. Summer sausage and cheese will be sliced for crackers, and fishing lures will be tied beneath a bright light and organized in the tackle box.

And the very next day, they will, at the least, provide a topic for conversation.

Weren't those mosquitoes bad last night?

Sure were, the kids were eaten alive.

We had to eat inside.

Us too. I don't think I've ever seen them bigger.

We played cards until midnight.

Us too, why don't you come over and play at our place tonight?

Well, that would be fun. We may as well stay inside if the mosquitoes are bad.

And so, on those nights when the mosquitoes are out in full force, it may do us well to consider that in order to not have mosquitoes, you need two things—no lakes and many, many bats.

In this case, maybe William Shakespeare said it best—Nothing in life is either good or bad, but thinking makes it so.

A pocket of late afternoon light says farewell to Lake Superior for the day.

This area of Minnesota's Lake Superior shoreline is home to famous Thompsonite stones.

FOR SOME PEOPLE, TO DREAM IS TO THINK ABOUT A LOG CABIN in the woods, where smoke curls soft and gray from a stone chimney and into a fresh blue sky. It is to dream about a place where wood for the fire is piled neatly outside the back door, where a white wooden rocking chair sits on the front porch, and where the smell of cedar or pine can make an entire house smell of the great outdoors.

It is to dream about a place in time that waits at the end of a long workweek, where red mittens and bright wool caps will hang by the fireplace to dry in the winter and where window panes will frame vases of garden flowers in the summer. It is to talk and plan and work for a house where the kitchen will always smell of apple and maple sugar, and friends drop by for a cup of coffee and a morning chat. In this dream, there is no television or telephone, just soft music from the radio, pouring out from the little log cabin in the woods.

Today, the term log cabin is used loosely to describe any type of log building. Theoretically, there are two different types, a log cabin and a log house. Log cabin usually means a simple, semi-permanent structure, something that is not finished in its entirety. Log house typically means a more permanent, finished structure with a sophisticated design.

For many, log construction seems as American as apple pie. Abraham Lincoln was born in one, and the wild frontier was dotted with them. In reality, log construction was brought to new America by northern and central European colonists. Other settlers learned from this, passing on their knowledge and experience as they settled new territories.

Later, other newcomers such as Swiss and German people brought their knowledge of log construction to America. As the frontier opened and settlers cleared land, most of them built cabins and gristmills, churches and schools out of log. Finally, when Scandinavian and Finnish settlers settled the upper Midwest, more log buildings and homes were built.

Whether it is to dream about a log house or cabin, these types of homes have seized the imaginations of many romantic souls, conjuring up images of peaceful shelters in the woods and rosy-cheeked youngsters picking apples or fishing from a nearby dock. Many cottage goers have been fortunate enough to enjoy this dream as a reality, while others wish, work, and wait, all the while planning for that up North getaway and enjoying the act of dreaming as much as the dream itself.

A classic log cabin.

A rusted hinge on the door of a primitive cabin.

Even the shovel is a classic at this cabin.

Silently, a broom lies in wait for the next clean up.

The stories that could be told from this lichen covered chair.

A wood stove warms the tea, the cabin and the heart.

Cross-country skis hang over the fireplace of a lodge-like cabin in northern Minnesota.

A Minnesota original...the hand hewn log cabin.

These logs seem to poke fun of the classic architecture.

THE LOON

THERE IS ONE VOICE THAT UNITES ALL PEOPLE WHO TRULY LOVE
the lake.

One voice that echoes above the silver-gold of morning, pene-
trating and mystifying the reeds and rushes that linger near.

It is one voice so ancient that it stirs in us all an inherited
knowledge of a wonder and mystery we all possess and yet somehow try to deny.

That is of course, until we hear its call, and are beckoned from
our beds and our breakfast tables to stand at the edge of the lake
and listen.

This is the very moment when true morning arrives, true
morning not of the day but of the spirit, when the loon wakes us
softly from our ancient dream sleep.

Sometimes, the sun has to battle for its sunrise.

At sunset, stones and boulders seem to eerily rise out from the lake to greet nightfall.

Lake Superior gently pounds its surf unto the shores of the Keweenaw Peninsula.

Evening sets upon a year-round cottage.

⊣ MADELINE ISLAND ⊢

WISCONSIN HAS AN ARCHIPELAGO OF 22 ISLANDS CALLED THE Apostle Islands. The largest of these is named Madeline.

The island was named for Madeline Cadotte, daughter of an Indian Chief, and eventually the wife of a fur trader.

The island was visited by Etienne Brule approximately the same time as the Pilgrims landed on Plymouth Rock. For 150 years or so, it was an important outpost for French, British, and American fur traders. When the Sault Locks opened in 1855, allowing easy passage to Lake Superior, the Apostle Islands began to host many newcomers.

Today, Madeline Island in the summer months has a population of approximately 2,500 people. For the 180 or so year-round residents, travel to the mainland is by ferryboat in summer, or ice road in winter. And on occasion, windsled.

The warmth from within the cottage radiates through the windows.

Yachting around Lake Superior's Apostle Islands makes for wonderful memories.

A glass table reflects window light upon a decorative boat.

Laid into the wood floor of this cottage is a compass denoting true north.

Morning dew is still evident on the glass decking of this log cottage.

The exterior of the log cottage is enhanced by several unique lanterns.

For the outdoorsman that lives in all of us.

A tribute to the northland woods is strewn throughout the cottage.

Fly fishing in the Great Lakes region is a religion to many anglers.

The Steelhead run comes into your favorite fishing hole on the river—and you are thinking—how lucky can I get?

Morning rises over this wonderful log cottage on a lake hidden from the rest of the world.

Sit on watermelon decorated stools while you have your morning coffee.

Outside, loons are calling, the sun is breaking through the fog, and it's time to go fishing for the one that always gets away.

A sailboat at rest near Sister Bay in Wisconsin's famous Door County Peninsula.

SAILING

A BUSY HARBOR IS A DELIGHT FOR THE SENSES. SINGLE MAST sloops with ropes flying in the wind, schooners budging their way into port—colorful sailcloth announcing the arrival of the busy time of year for many port stops.

The first sailing craft on the Great Lakes date back to ships constructed on Lake Ontario in the 1600s. It was the Griffin, built by Rene-Robert Cavelier, Sieur de LaSalle in 1670 above Niagara Falls that launched navigation on the upper Great Lakes.

No matter what type of boat you command, no matter where you are going or who you are bringing along, every sailor into port has plied the same water, felt the same current, and had the same wind on their face.

The best transportation for a sailor beyond his sailboat is the summer cruiser bike.

DOOR COUNTY PENINSULA

DOOR PENINSULA IS AN 85 MILE LONG PIECE OF LAND IN northeastern Wisconsin that extends out into Lake Michigan. Upon its 250 miles or more of shoreline are cottages and villages that echo the sentiments of nostalgic cottage life. The bays, the fishing villages, the cherries and the plum orchards all give rise to pictures in our imaginations, where women still walk around wearing clam-diggers and rubber boots, where children still ride simple red bicycles with brown paper bags of store candy in their grasp, and where a stringer of fish and a couple of potatoes are the perfect summertime dinner for a family of four.

Craggy rocks embrace much of the Door County Peninsula.

This cottage is nestled deep into the wooded shoreline of Lake Michigan.

Aqua water beckons.

You drive for many hours and you come to the trail's end, and this dock answers every reason why you came.

The classic construction of this cottage leaves a lasting impression.

Dovetail joints graciously meet at each corner of this log cottage.

Incredible log construction compliments the rugged shoreline of Michigan's Upper Peninsula.

CRAFTSMANSHIP

SOME LOG CABINS TODAY, AS ON THE NORTH SHORE OF LAKE Superior, were made from Finnish settlers who truly knew how to use the land and its resources.

Basically, plan and form were the two most important thoughts to these early structures. Sometimes corner notching varied by culture.

Saddle notching, steeple and full dovetail notching, all add to the vocabulary and aura of the quiet and sturdy structure of these settlers.

Everything should be right. The lights should glow in all the right places, the windows should angle amidst the woods just so. Each corner should be fluid and strong and a picture of beauty itself.

Flawless corners come together on this hand built log cottage.

AUTUMN

THE AUTUMN TREESCAPE VIBRATES WITH COLOR—RICH SHADES of red and lemon-yellow wave back and forth against a caramel colored hillside. In the Great Lakes area, just before the cold snap closes in, inland lakes become dark and turn from deep blue to gray to black. As the season changes from soft summer-green to fall, the sound of car doors opening and closing is less frequent, the mornings become quieter, and stories start to circulate about who is going where and doing what for the winter.

But autumn, for those who are fortunate enough to experience it in the Lakes area, is an in-between time, an afterlife of sorts where days on end can be spent exploring—just looking around. These are the stolen moments when a fishing boat is captured, a thermos of coffee is prepared, and a sweater buttoned up for the ride. And as solitude is sought and found in a half-moon bay of reeds and rushes and sweet lake grasses, it is inviting to do nothing but stop your life.

And just look around.

That's all. Just to look around and spot minnows as they huddle and then scatter in the shallows, to watch with envy as herons stretch one last time before winter calls them elsewhere. To watch wavelets as they flow. To sip coffee and admire the handiwork of a greater being. To listen to geese as they fly overhead, and to smell the decay of the nearby forest while the leaves float down like confetti.

Simply, to be in your boat and to just look around—while the world that's preparing for winter—just beyond the shore—must wait.

Autumn lingers upon a northern Minnesota lake.

Through thick birches lies a unique and rare cordwood cottage.

Home to a passionate carver, as seen by the small detail carving on the outside of the cottage.

The interesting exterior of artistic cordwood walls.

Open and spacious, this cottage was meant for many children, grandchildren and guests.

Stocked with history, this cottage stands timeless on a small inland lake.

Poised and waiting for its daily trip around the lake.

┤ THE BOAT RIDE ├

THERE ARE MANY THINGS YOU WOULD LIKE TO DO INSIDE. Have tea with your spouse, read books to your children, or perhaps your children's children, or even just fix the kitchen sink.

That is what your heart wants you to do. That is what your heart tells you is best to do.

And that would be fine.

Yes, that would be fine if it weren't for your soul.

Ah, your soul. It has another idea.

It pushes you out the door and down to the dock, where your life jacket waits. You can barely help grinning as you step into your boat.

And take a ride.

Even if it's only for a few minutes. Take a ride and let the wind pulse against your face and toss your hair into strands of disorder, let it enter your body as you look around at the passing shore, a blur of blue and green and shades of tan.

And for a little while, you let your heart and soul play tag with each other while you ride beyond the bays. There is always time to turn around. Just not yet.

A classic painting of the region hangs proudly on the cottage wall.

IN FRENCH LANGUAGE, LES CHENEAUX MEANS "THE CHANNELS."
Thirty-six islands that form a waterway twelve miles long on the
north coast of Lake Huron is the area of the Les Cheneaux Islands.

The islands create quiet coves and sheltered bays, and with its
wonderful rocky maze of water trails, there is natural protection
from the winds, making it a calm and peaceful place to navigate
small watercraft.

Boat racks lay dormant now that the summer visitors are gone.

Many classic cruising boats run about the islands of the Les Cheneaux area.

Many old cruising boats are being preserved by local artisans in this island area to keep its rich boating history alive.

┤ LES CHENEAUX ├

MANY OF THE COTTAGES OF THE LES CHENEAUX AREA ARE ON islands, and boaters can be seen steering the refinished wooden boats gently through the islands, and to the shore, or back again. It is a lifestyle that is as much about the boat as it is the cottage.

An archway on the dock makes for a timeless entrance.

Inside the main cottage is an expansive living room that has entertained guests for many years.

A cottage on one of the dozens of islands that comprise the Les Cheneaux islands area is a masterful tribute to cottage life in Michigan's Upper Peninsula.

The day's end is met by the glow from this log cottage in Michigan's rugged Upper Peninsula.

A magnificent fireplace that appears to reach for the stars.

Guests are welcomed by a vintage rustic wintertime display.

Christmastime in a cottage—crackling fires, deep winter snows and lots of warm cocoa.

IT'S A WONDERFUL LIFE

TO WALK ON A WINTER PATH AND LET SNOWFLAKES LAND ON your tongue. To make snow angels in the woods when only the spruce and pine trees are watching. To sit on a snowy log and watch stars poke out from behind the edges of dark winter clouds. To listen to an owl. To call out to your dog.

Yes, it's a wonderful life.

And it's not about material possessions. It's not about cars. It's not about homes. And it's definitely not about money.

It's about coming home and being warmed by a gentle fire of the spirit. It's about pulling off your boots and not caring if you step into a cold puddle of melted snow because there are other warm socks waiting for you. It's about having time to sit by the hearth and wait for your longjohns to dry because there is nowhere you have to be. It's about being able to afford nothing more than hot cocoa and marshmallows on a cold Saturday night when your children are young. It's about being thankful for what you have, and for the beauty of all that surrounds you.

Indeed, it is a wonderful, wonderful life.

⊣ ACKNOWLEDGMENTS ⊢

WE WOULD LIKE TO GENEROUSLY THANK ALL OF THE WONDER-ful people who helped us with the project—from Ontario, Canada and throughout all of the Great Lake states. Your passion for cottage life inspired us—and the magic of each place was contagious. Special mention should go out to the Wallin and Gagnon families and to Kay Cartford and Betty Lessard for their extra support of this project. As well, we would like to thank Julie Norcross of McLean & Eakin Booksellers in Petoskey, Michigan, Barb Siepkar of the Cottage Bookshop in Glen Arbor, Rick Baron, the Northlander and its crew, Tim Casey and Ted Gregg of Northern Visions Inc., Mark and Gail Dreisbach, Stephan Biggs, Fred Ball, Holly Young, Mike Dorn, John Faegre, Bill Carlson and family, Phyllis and Jennifer Gardner, Mary Tobash, Jeff and Janet Hessler of Betsie Bay Furniture, Dwight and Barbara Reed, Frida Waara of On-Cue Productions, the Grutzmachers at Passtimes Books, the Hawley family, Jan McCray, Bob Humphrey, the folks at Nautical by the Bay in Harbor Springs Michigan and an extra thank you to all of the cottage owners who opened their hearts and their homes to us during this project.

In addition on the technical side, a special thank you must go to Mike Lussier of AGX Imaging labs for his excellence in film processing and to Daniel McGuire of Kodak for his continued help and support of my projects. As well, to Wayne Hodgson of Muskoka North & Film of Canada, to Image Arts for their dedication to quality, to Pat Goodall from Westphoto for his technical support and finally, to our friends and families and to Sleeping Bear Press for all of their vision and support on this project.

PHOTOGRAPHER ED WARGIN AND AUTHOR KATHY-JO WARGIN collaborated on *The Great Lakes Cottage Book* because of their love for cottage and cabin nostalgia. Ed and Kathy-jo were originally from northern Minnesota, where small inland lakes and cabin life created wonderful memories for them both. Ed has more than 15 years experience in commercial photography. He specializes in working on location in natural light as well as shooting extensively for his fine art collection. Kathy-jo has written several children's books including the award-winning *The Legend of Sleeping Bear* and *The Legend of Mackinac Island*, as well as the newly released *The Legend of the Loon*. As a couple, they created the coffeetable book, *Michigan, The Spirit of the Land*. They reside in northern Michigan in a little brown house in the woods.